The Birthday Book

Floral designs
Jane Newdick

Photography
Full-page photographs: Neil Sutherland
Cut-out photographs: Paul Turner and Sue Pressley,
   Stonecastle Graphics Ltd

Design
Paul Turner and Sue Pressley, Stonecastle Graphics Ltd

Editorial
Jo Finnis
David Squire
Robyn Bryant

Published 1992 by
Tormont Publications Inc.
338 Saint-Antoine St. East
Montreal, Quebec, Canada H2Y 1A3
Tel. (514) 954-1441 Fax (514) 954-1443

Printed in U.S.A.

The Birthday Book

Birthdays, Anniversaries and Special Days to Remember

TORMONT

January

Birthstone: garnet

By her who in this month is born,
No gems save garnets should be worn;
They will insure her constancy,
True friendship and fidelity.

ANON

January

1
New Year's Day

1735 Birth of Paul Revere, American patriot

1863 Birth of Baron Pierre de Coubertin, founder of the modern Olympics

1895 Birth of J Edgar Hoover, founder of the FBI

2

1920 Birth of Isaac Asimov, Russian-born biochemist and science fiction writer

3

1892 Birth of J R Tolkien, British writer, author of *The Hobbit* and *Lord of the Rings*

1909 Birth of Victor Borge, Danish-born comedian and pianist

4

5

1896 First demonstration of X-rays

1946 Birth of Diane Keaton, American actress

Epiphany

6
Twelfth night

And going into the house they saw the child with Mary his mother, and they fell down and worshipped him. Then, opening their treasures, they offered him gifts, gold and frankincense and myrrh.
MATTHEW II, 11

7

1925 Birth of Gerald Durrell, English naturalist and author

January

Polarity: Capricorn is a negative or feminine sign. These signs have a self-repressive and passive tendency.

8

1935 Birth of Elvis Presley, American singer

1947 Birth of David Bowie, British musician and actor

9

1908 Birth of French writer Simone de Beauvoir, author of *The Second Sex*

1913 Birth of Richard Nixon, 37th president of the USA

10

1918 The US House of Representatives voted in favor of women's suffrage

1945 Birth of Rod Stewart, British singer-songwriter

11

12

*In happy homes he saw the light
Of household fires gleam warm and
bright.*

H W LONGFELLOW

13

14

1941 Birth of Faye Dunaway, American actress

A warm January, a cold May.

WELSH PROVERB

January

15

16

17

1706 Birth of Benjamin Franklin, American scientist and statesman

1942 Birth of Muhammad Ali, American boxer

18

1904 Birth of Cary Grant, British-born American film actor

1913 Birth of Danny Kaye, film and stage actor

19

1839 Birth of Paul Cézanne, French painter

1946 Birth of Dolly Parton, American country singer

20

1896 Birth of George Burns, American comedian

1910 Birth of Joy Adamson, German-born author and conservationist

Marry when the year is new,
Always loving, always true.   ANON

21

1926 Birth of Telly Savalas, American actor

1940 Birth of Jack Nicklaus, American golfer

1941 Birth of Placido Domingo, Spanish-born operatic tenor

January

AQUARIUS
21 January - 18 February
Aquarians are true humanitarians possessing a deep social conscience. They are highly self-controlled so can appear cool and detached, but their emotional natures are complex.

22

1788 Birth of Lord Byron, English poet

1940 Birth of John Hurt, British actor

23

24

25

1759 Birth of Robert Burns, Scottish poet

1882 Birth of Virginia Woolf, British writer

26

1925 Birth of Paul Newman, American film actor

27

1756 Birth of Wolfgang Amadeus Mozart, Austrian composer

1832 Birth of Lewis Carroll (Charles Lutwidge Dodgson) author of *Alice in Wonderland*

1942 Birth of Mikhail Baryshnikov, Russian-born ballet dancer

28

1873 Birth of Colette (Gabrielle Sidonie), French novelist

1936 Birth of Alan Alda, American actor and director

1912 Birth of Jackson Pollock, American painter

January

29

1880 Birth of W C Fields, American comic actor

1939 Birth of Germaine Greer, Australian feminist and writer

1945 Birth of Tom Selleck, American actor

30

1931 Birth of Gene Hackman, American actor

1937 Birth of Vanessa Redgrave, British actress

31

1797 Birth of Franz Schubert, Austrian composer

Fragrant flower basket
Fill a shallow basket with a selection of dried flowers that offers a rich tapestry of color and texture: red and pink roses, hydrangea, deep blue larkspur, sprigs of lavender and poppy seedheads. Set the stalks in a piece of dry oasis to enable you to create the overall shape of the arrangement that you want. Enhance the natural fragrance of the flowers by adding a few drops of rose essential oil.

Fragrant fires
Tie together the dried stems of lavender, rosemary, thyme and lemon verbena to form bundles which you can then add to your winter fire to create a heart-warming aroma.

February

Birthstone: amethyst

The February born will find
Sincerity and peace of mind;
Freedom from passion and from care
If they the amethyst will wear.

ANON

February

Element: Aquarius is an air sign. Air signs are mentally active, rational and communicative.

1

1901 Birth of Clark Gable, American film actor

1931 Birth of Boris Yeltsin, Russian politician

2

Groundhog Day

1650 Birth of Nell Gwyn, actress and mistress of King Charles II

1882 Birth of James Joyce, Irish novelist

1927 Birth of Stan Getz, American jazz saxophonist

3

4

5

1900 Birth of Adlai Stevenson II, US statesman and UN ambassador

1945 Birth of Bob Marley, Jamaican reggae musician

6

1911 Birth of Ronald Reagan, 40th president of the USA

Rain in February is as good as manure.
FRENCH PROVERB

7

1812 Birth of Charles Dickens, British novelist

February

Quadruplicity: Aquarius is a fixed sign. These signs are steadfast sustainers.

8

1925 Birth of Jack Lemmon, American film actor

1931 Birth of James Dean, American film actor

9

1945 Birth of Mia Farrow, American film actress

10

1890 Birth of Boris Pasternak, Russian author of *Dr Zhivago*

1893 Birth of Jimmy Durante, US comedian and vaudeville performer

11

1847 Birth of Thomas Alva Edison, American inventor

1936 Birth of Burt Reynolds, American film actor

12

1809 Birth of Charles Darwin, British naturalist

13

14

Saint Valentine's Day

O my luve's like a red, red rose
That's newly sprung in June;
O my luve's like the melodie
That's sweetly play'd in tune.
ROBERT BURNS

 # February

1564 Birth of Galileo, Italian astronomer and scientist

15

16

1923 Inner tomb of King Tutankhamun opened in Egypt

1930 Birth of Ruth Rendell, British novelist

17

1934 Birth of Alan Bates, British actor

1954 Birth of John Travolta, American film actor

18

1924 Birth of Lee Marvin, American film actor

19

1960 Birth of Prince Andrew, Duke of York

1927 Birth of Sydney Poitier, American film actor

20

1934 Birth of Nina Simone, American jazz singer

21

February

22

1732 Birth of George Washington, first US President

1932 Birth of Edward Kennedy, US senator

23

1633 Birth of Samuel Pepys, English diarist and civil servant

1685 Birth of George Frederick Handel, German composer

24

1887 Paris and Brussels became the first two cities to be linked by telephone

1932 Birth of Michel Legrand, French composer and conductor

25

1873 Birth of Enrico Caruso, Italian singer

1943 Birth of George Harrison, British songwriter and performer, member of *The Beatles*

26

1932 Birth of Johnny Cash, American country singer

If February give much snow,
A fine summer it doth foreshow.
ENGLISH RHYME

27

28/29

March

Birthstone: aquamarine or bloodstone

Who in this world of ours their eyes
In March first open shall be wise;
In days of peril firm and brave,
And wear a bloodstone to their grave.

ANON

March

1

1904 Birth of Glenn Miller, American composer and trombonist

2

3

1911 Birth of Jean Harlow, American film actress

1931 Birth of Mikhail Gorbachev, Russian politician

4

1678 Birth of Vivaldi, Italian composer and violinist

1931 Birth of Miriam Makeba, South African singer

5

1908 Birth of Rex Harrison, British actor

March comes in like a lion and goes out like a lamb.

ENGLISH PROVERB

6

1475 Birth of Michelangelo, Italian Renaissance painter

1806 Birth of Elizabeth Barrett Browning, English poet

1944 Birth of Dame Kiri Te Kanawa, New Zealand opera singer

7

1872 Birth of Piet Mondrian, Dutch abstract painter

1875 Birth of Maurice Ravel, French composer

1960 Birth of Ivan Lendl, Czech tennis player

March

8

9

1876 Alexander Graham Bell made the first telephone call

10

11

1916 Birth of Harold Wilson, British Prime Minister

1931 Birth of Rupert Murdoch, Australian-born American newspaper publisher

12

1946 Birth of Liza Minnelli, American actress and singer

1961 Yuri Gagarin became the first man in space

13

1930 Discovery of the planet Pluto announced by American astronomer, Clyde Tombaugh

14

1879 Birth of Albert Einstein, German physicist

1933 Birth of Michael Caine, British actor

March

22

1930 Birth of Stephen Sondheim, US composer and lyricist

1931 Birth of William Shatner, Canadian actor

1948 Birth of Andrew Lloyd Webber, British composer

23

1908 Birth of Joan Crawford, American movie actress

Spring makes everything young again, save man.

JEAN PAUL RICHTER

24

1834 Birth of William Morris, British artist and craftsman

1930 Birth of Steve McQueen, American film actor

25

1947 Birth of Elton John, British musician and composer

26

1931 Birth of Leonard Nimoy, American actor and director

1944 Birth of Diana Ross, American singer and actress

27

28

1483 Birth of Raphael, Italian painter

March

29

1886 First batch of *Coca-Cola* brewed

1918 Birth of Pearl Bailey, US jazz singer

1943 Birth of John Major, British Prime Minister

30

1853 Birth of Van Gogh, Dutch painter

1937 Birth of Warren Beatty, American film actor

1945 Birth of Eric Clapton, British guitarist and songwriter

31

1732 Birth of Franz Joseph Haydn, Austrian composer

1934 Birth of Shirley Jones, American actress

Easter biscuits
1¾ cups (450 mL) flour
½ tsp (2 mL) salt
1 level tsp (5 mL) ground cinnamon
⅓ cup (75 mL) currants or raisins
⅔ cup (150 mL) butter or margarine
⅔ cup (150 mL) superfine sugar
1 egg yolk (reserve egg white for glazing)

Preheat the oven to 350° F (180° C). Mix the flour, salt and cinnamon together, then add the dried fruit. Beat the butter or margarine until soft, add sugar, and cream together until fluffy. Gradually beat in egg yolk. Fold in flour mixture using a knife, then the fingers. Knead on a lightly-floured surface and roll out to ¼ in (6 mm) thick. Cut into 2 in (5 cm) rounds with a cookie cutter. Prick the surface of biscuits with a fork. Place on a greased baking tray and bake for 15 minutes. Remove pan from oven, brush biscuits with beaten egg white, and sprinkle with fine sugar. Return to oven for another 5 minutes.

April

Birthstone: diamond

She who from April dates her years,
Diamonds should wear, lest bitter tears
For vain repentance flow; this stone,
Emblem of innocence is known.

ANON

April

1

The first day of April,
You may send a fool whither you will.
THOMAS FULLER

April Fools' Day

2

1725 Birth of Giovanni Giacomo Casanova, notorious Italian adventurer

1914 Birth of Sir Alec Guinness, British actor

1947 Birth of Emmylou Harris, American singer

3

1924 Birth of Doris Day, American actress and singer

1924 Birth of Marlon Brando, American actor

1961 Birth of Eddie Murphy, American film actor

4

At Easter let your clothes be new
Or else be sure you will it rue.
OLD ENGLISH RHYME

5

1908 Birth of Bette Davis, American actress

1916 Birth of Gregory Peck, American actor

6

7

1915 Birth of Billie Holiday, American singer

1928 Birth of James Garner, American actor

April

8

1893 Birth of Mary Pickford, Canadian-born movie actress

Loveliest of trees, the cherry now
Is hung with bloom along the bough,
And stands about the woodland ride
Wearing white for Eastertide.

A E HOUSEMAN

9

1933 Birth of Jean-Paul Belmondo, French actor

10

1903 Birth of Clare Booth Luce, US playwright, politician and ambassador

1932 Birth of Omar Sharif, Egyptian actor

11

12

1923 Birth of Maria Callas, American-born Greek opera diva

13

1866 Birth of Butch Cassidy, American outlaw

1906 Birth of Samuel Beckett, Irish playwright

14

1904 Birth of Sir John Gielgud, British actor and theatrical producer

1932 Birth of Anthony Perkins, American film actor

1940 Birth of Julie Christie, English actress

April

15

1894 Birth of Bessie Smith, American blues singer

April showers do bring May flowers.
THOMAS TUSSER

16

1889 Birth of Charlie Chaplin, British-born American actor and director

1918 Birth of Spike Milligan, British actor and author

1921 Birth of Peter Ustinov, British dramatist and actor

17

18

19

1935 Birth of Dudley Moore, British film actor, composer, and musician

20

1889 Birth of Adolf Hitler, German dictator

21

1926 Birth of Queen Elizabeth II

April

TAURUS
21 April - 21 May
Taureans are seekers of peace and stability. Unambitious, they are quite happy to be the powerhouse behind the scenes. They are sensible and healthily cynical, but also possess a gentle facet.

22

1916 Birth of Yehudi Menuhin, American-born British violinist

1922 Birth of Charles Mingus, US jazz innovator and bandleader

1937 Birth of Jack Nicholson, American actor and film maker

23

1775 Birth of J M W Turner, English painter

1564 Birth of William Shakespeare, English poet, dramatist and actor

24

1905 Birth of Robert Penn Warren, US poet and author

1934 Birth of Shirley MacLaine, American actress

1942 Birth of Barbra Streisand, American film actress and singer

25

1918 Birth of Ella Fitzgerald, US jazz singer

1940 Birth of Al Pacino, American film actor

26

1785 Birth of John James Audubon, US naturalist and artist

1936 Birth of Carol Burnett, US comedienne

27

28

1941 Birth of Ann-Margret, Swedish-born American actress

April

Polarity: Taurus is a negative or feminine sign. These signs have a self-repressive and passive tendency.

29

1863 Birth of William Randolph Hearst, US newspaper magnate

1899 Birth of Duke Ellington, US composer, pianist and bandleader

30

1789 George Washington inaugurated as first president of the USA

Crystallized flowers
To crystallize edible flowers such as primroses and violets, beat an egg white until it is no longer glutinous. Using a small fine paintbrush, paint the egg white lightly and evenly onto both upper and lower surfaces of the flowers. Sprinkle some superfine sugar immediately and evenly over each flower, then shake off any excess. Leave to dry on waxed paper for at least 2 hours. As well as making delightful decorations for a celebration cake, crystallized primroses, violets, borage, auriculas, pear and cherry blossoms are all scrumptious!

Marshmallow flowers
To make daisies, dip scissors into water and form four petals by cutting across the flat side of a marshmallow. Cut out five petals and arrange them on waxed paper, overlapping slightly, to make a flower design. Using food colorings, color some sugar yellow and some green. Dip the inside of each flower in the yellow sugar, coating the cut sides of the petals. Use a small piece of marshmallow to make the daisy centers. To make leaves, dip single petals into the green sugar.

May

Birthstone: emerald

Who first beholds the light of day
In Spring's sweet flowery month of May
And wears an emerald all her life,
Shall be a loved and happy wife.

ANON

May

1

1916 Birth of Glenn Ford, Canadian-born actor

1931 Empire State Building opened in New York

2

1901 Birth of Bing Crosby, American singer and film actor

3

4

5

1929 Birth of Audrey Hepburn, American actress

1818 Birth of Karl Marx, German political theorist, sociologist and economist

1961 Alan B Shepard became the first US astronaut in space

6

1856 Birth of Sigmund Freud, Austrian psychiatrist and father of psychoanalysis

1895 Birth of Rudolph Valentino, Italian-born American film actor

1915 Birth of Orson Welles, US actor and film director

7

1840 Birth of Piotr Ilyich Tchaikovsky, Russian composer

And May was come, the month of gladness.

JOHN LYDGATE

May

8

1926 Birth of Sir David Attenborough, British broadcaster and writer

1940 Birth of Peter Benchley, US author of *Jaws*

9

1910 Birth of Barbara Woodhouse, Irish-born dog trainer and television celebrity

1920 Birth of Richard Adams, English author of *Watership Down*

1936 Birth of Glenda Jackson, British actress

10

1899 Birth of Fred Astaire, American dancer and entertainer

1946 Birth of Donovan, Scottish guitarist, singer and songwriter

11

1888 Birth of Irving Berlin, American composer

1904 Birth of Salvador Dali, Spanish painter

12

1820 Birth of Florence Nightingale, English nurse and hospital reformer

1929 Birth of Burt Bacharach, US composer

13

14

May

15

1909 Birth of James Mason, British actor

16

1905 Birth of Henry Fonda, American film actor

1919 Birth of Liberace, US pianist and entertainer

17

May is the month to marry bad wives.
LATIN PROVERB

18

1919 Birth of Margot Fonteyn, British ballerina

1920 Birth of Pope John Paul II (Karol Wojtyla)

19

1939 Birth of James Fox, British actor

1946 Birth of Candice Bergen, American actress and photo-journalist

20

1908 Birth of James Stewart, American film actor

21

May

22

1859 Birth of Sir Arthur Conan Doyle,
British writer, creator of Sherlock
Holmes

1907 Birth of Sir Laurence Olivier,
British actor, director and producer

23

1933 Birth of Joan Collins, British
actress and novelist

1951 Birth of Anatoliy Karpov, Russian
chess player

24

1819 Birth of Queen Victoria

1941 Birth of Bob Dylan, American
composer and singer

25

1926 Birth of Miles Davis, US jazz
trumpeter

26

27

1911 Birth of Vincent Price, American
film actor

1923 Birth of Henry Kissinger, US
Secretary of State and winner of Nobel
Peace Prize

28

1908 Birth of Ian Fleming, British
novelist, creator of James Bond

1967 Sir Francis Chichester completed
round the world solo yacht trip

May

Polarity: Gemini is a positive or masculine sign. These signs have a self-expressive and spontaneous tendency.

29

1903 Birth of Bob Hope, British-born American comedian and actor

1917 Birth of J F Kennedy, 35th president of the USA

1953 Everest scaled by Hillary and Tensing

30

A dry May and a leaking June
Make the farmer whistle a merry tune.
OLD ENGLISH RHYME

31

1923 Birth of Prince Rainier III of Monaco

1930 Birth of Clint Eastwood, American film actor and director

A draught of fragrance
For a perfect early summer gift, fill a cut-glass goblet with a posy of heavenly-scented flowers . The delicate bells of the lily of the valley are exquisitely fragrant, while honeysuckle has a warm, sweet scent.

June

Birthstone: agate, pearl, moonstone or alexandrite

Who comes with Summer to this earth
And owes to June her day of birth
With ring of agate on her hand,
Can health, wealth, and long life command.

ANON

June

1

1926 Birth of Marilyn Monroe, American film actress

1938 *Superman*, created by two US college students, made his first comic book flight

2

1840 Birth of Thomas Hardy, British poet and novelist

1944 Birth of Marvin Hamlisch, US composer of *A Chorus Line*

3

1925 Birth of Tony Curtis, American film actor

4

5

1942 Birth of Tammy Wynette, American singer

6

1956 Birth of Bjorn Borg, Swedish tennis player

What is so rare as a day in June?
Then, if ever, come perfect days.
J R LOWELL

7

1940 Birth of Tom Jones, Welsh singer

1958 Birth of Prince, American singer, musician and actor

June

Quadruplicity: Gemini is a mutable sign. These signs are changeable and supremely adaptable.

8

1810 Birth of Robert Schumann, German composer

9

1892 Birth of Cole Porter, American composer and lyricist

1961 Birth of Michael J Fox, American film actor

10

1921 Birth of Prince Philip, Duke of Edinburgh

1922 Birth of Judy Garland, American singer and actress

11

1776 Birth of John Constable, English painter

1910 Birth of Jacques Cousteau, French marine explorer, writer and film producer

1939 Birth of Jackie Stewart, Scottish racing driver

12

1667 First blood transfusion administered

1924 Birth of George Bush, 41st president of the USA

1929 Birth of Anne Frank, Jewish diarist

13

14

June

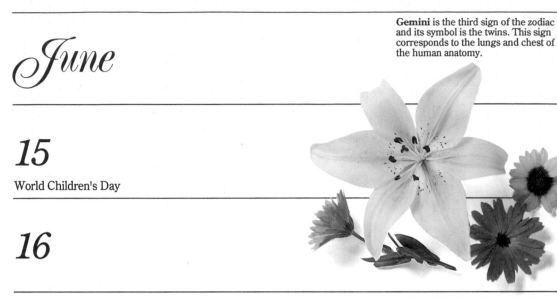

15

World Children's Day

16

17

1882 Birth of Igor Stravinsky, Russian composer

1917 Birth of Dean Martin, American film actor and singer

1950 The first kidney transplant was performed in Chicago

18

1942 Birth of Paul McCartney, British songwriter, singer and musician, member of *The Beatles*

1978 Comic strip cat *Garfield* was created

19

1947 Birth of Salman Rushdie, British writer

1954 Birth of Kathleen Turner, American film actress

20

1909 Birth of Errol Flynn, Australian-born American film actor

21

1905 Birth of Jean-Paul Sartre, French philosopher

1912 Birth of Mary McCarthy, US novelist

June

CANCER
22 June - 22 July
Cancers value their security, enjoying the safety and comfort of the familiar. They are emotionally vulnerable and so take steps to protect themselves. They make excellent conciliators.

22

1936 Birth of Kris Kristofferson, American singer, songwriter and actor

1949 Birth of Meryl Streep, American film actress

23

1763 Birth of Josephine, who married Napoleon

1927 Birth of Bob Fosse, US choreographer and director

24

On a morn in June
When the dew glistens on the pearled ears,
A shiver runs through the deep corn for
joy.
MATTHEW ARNOLD

Saint John the Baptist's Day

25

1903 Birth of George Orwell, English novelist
1945 Birth of Carly Simon, US singer and songwriter
1963 Birth of George Michael, British singer, composer and producer

26

27

28

1902 Birth of Richard Rodgers, US composer and lyricist

1926 Birth of Mel Brooks, American film writer, producer and director

June

29

1956 Marilyn Monroe married playwright, Arthur Miller

30

*Give me a glut of strawberries; and lo!
Sweet through my blood, and very bones,
they go.*

LEIGH HUNT, TRANSLATED FROM AN
UNIDENTIFIED ITALIAN POET

Strawberry treats
25 strawberries with tops, washed and
  dried
6oz (¾ cup or 170g) plain (dark)
  chocolate broken into pieces
1 or 2 tbsp (15 or 30 mL) shortening

Melt chocolate and shortening in the
top of a double boiler over low heat.
Remove from heat. With a skewer, spear
one strawberry at a time through the
leaf part and dip the bottom half of the
fruit into the melted chocolate. Carefully
remove from the skewer and leave
to cool on waxed paper. Place in petit-
four cases, cover and store in the
refrigerator. A mouth-watering
summertime gift!

July

Birthstone: ruby

The glowing ruby should adorn
Those who in warm July are born,
Then will they be exempt and free
From love's doubt and anxiety.

ANON

July

Element: Cancer is a water sign. These signs are artistic, emotional and perceptive.

1961 Birth of Diana, the Princess of Wales

1
Canada Day

2

3

1937 Birth of Tom Stoppard, Czech-born English playwright

1776 Independence Day, USA

1927 Birth of Neil Simon, American playwright

1927 Birth of Gina Lollobrigida, Italian actress

4
Independence Day (US)

Hot July brings cooling showers,
Apricots and gillyflowers.
SARA COLERIDGE

5

1935 Birth of the Dalai Lama, 14th spiritual leader of Tibet

1946 Birth of Sylvester Stallone, American film actor and director

6

1887 Birth of Marc Chagall, Russian-born painter

1940 Birth of Ringo Starr, British entertainer and member of *The Beatles*

7

July

Quadruplicity: Cancer is a cardinal sign. These signs are enterprising instigators.

8

Essence of roses
Take 2 cups distilled water, 2 cups strongly-scented rose petals and ¾ cup vodka. Mix ingredients together well. Leave for several days, covered. Strain off liquid and add a few drops of rose oil if desired.

9

1901 Birth of Barbara Cartland, British novelist and playwright

1916 Birth of Edward Heath, British Prime Minister

1937 Birth of David Hockney, British artist

10

11

12

1817 Birth of Henry David Thoreau, US author and naturalist

1937 Birth of Bill Cosby, US comedian and actor

1942 Birth of Harrison Ford, American film actor

13

14

1903 Birth of Irving Stone, US novelist

1912 Birth of Woody Guthrie, legendary US folk singer

1918 Birth of Ingmar Bergman, Swedish film writer-director

July

Cancer is the fourth sign of the zodiac and its symbol is the crab. This sign corresponds to the breasts and stomach of the human anatomy.

15

16

17

1899 Birth of James Cagney, American film actor

1935 Birth of Donald Sutherland, Canadian actor

18

1918 Birth of Nelson Mandela, South African politician

1955 Disneyland opened in Los Angeles, USA

19

1834 Birth of Edgar Degas, French Impressionist painter

1946 Birth of Ilie Nastase, Romanian tennis player

20

1938 Birth of Diana Rigg, British actress

21

1899 Birth of Ernest Hemingway, American writer

1969 Neil Armstrong became the first man to set foot on the moon

July

22

Herb cheese spread
Take 2 tbsp (30ml) chopped parsley, 1 tbsp (15ml) chopped chives, 8oz (1 cup or 225g) soft cheese, juice of 1 lemon and salt and black pepper. Beat the herbs into the cheese, then add lemon juice and seasoning. Mix until smooth. Chill.

23

1888 Birth of Raymond Chandler, American mystery writer

24

Laws of gardening:
1. Other people's tools work only in other people's gardens. 2. Fancy gizmos don't work. 3. If nobody uses it, there's a reason. 4. You get the most of what you need the least.
ARTHUR BLOCH

25

1894 Birth of Walter Brennan, US film actor

1943 Birth of Mick Jagger, British vocalist, songwriter and actor

26

1856 Birth of George Bernard Shaw, British writer

27

28

July

29

1883 Birth of Benito Mussolini, Italian dictator

1981 Marriage of Prince Charles and Lady Diana Spencer

30

1863 Birth of Henry Ford, American motor car manufacturer

1947 Birth of Arnold Schwarzenegger, Austrian-born American film actor

31

1944 Birth of Geraldine Chaplin, American actress

Flower-scented teas

Add 2 tbsp sweet summer jasmine flowerheads to every $1/2$lb (1 cup or 250g) large-leaf China tea. Alternatively, substitute rose petals for the jasmine to make a deliciously fragrant and refreshing variation. These special perfumed teas will make unusual and attractive gifts. Present the teas in their own decorative boxes, either wooden or tin, finished off with some pretty ribbon.

August

Birthstone: peridot or sardonyx

Wear a sardonyx or for thee
No conjugal felicity.
The August-born without this stone
'Tis said must live unloved and lone.

ANON

August

Element: Leo is a fire sign. These signs are enthusiastic, energetic and assertive.

1

1936 Birth of Yves Saint-Laurent, French couturier

Any colour, so long as it's red
Is the colour that suits me best.
                                    EUGENE FIELD

2

1924 Birth of James Baldwin, American author

1932 Birth of Peter O'Toole, Irish actor

3

4

1900 Birth of Queen Elizabeth, the Queen Mother

5

1930 Birth of Neil Armstrong, American astronaut and professor of engineering

6

1881 Birth of Alexander Fleming, Scottish bacteriologist who discovered penicillin

1917 Birth of Robert Mitchum, American actor

7

I've had enough of gardening - I'm just about ready to throw in the trowel.
                                    ANON

August

8

1937 Birth of Dustin Hoffman, American actor

1974 Richard Nixon became the first US President to resign

9

*I'll say she looks as clear
As morning roses newly wash'd with dew*
SHAKESPEARE

10

11

12

1881 Birth of Cecil B De Mille, US film producer and director

13

1899 Birth of Alfred Hitchcock, British-born American film director

1927 Birth of Fidel Castro, Cuban politician

14

1867 Birth of John Galsworthy, author of *The Forsyte Saga*

1947 Birth of Danielle Steele, American writer

August

15

1769 Birth of Napoléon Bonaparte, French emperor

1888 Birth of T E Lawrence (Lawrence of Arabia)

1925 Birth of Oscar Peterson, Canadian jazz pianist

16

The blue of distance, however intense, is not the blue of a bright blue flower.
JOHN RUSKIN

17

1786 Birth of Davy Crockett, American frontiersman and politician

1892 Birth of Mae West, American film actress

1943 Birth of Robert DeNiro, American film actor

18

1937 Birth of Robert Redford, American film actor

19

1883 Birth of Coco Chanel, French fashion designer

1902 Birth of Ogden Nash, American humorist and lyricist

20

21

1904 Birth of Count Basie, American pianist and composer

1959 Hawaii became the 50th US state

August

VIRGO
24 August - 23 September
Virgos value knowledge highly. They make good teachers and advisers, while avoiding positions of prominent power. Often shy, Virgos hide their sensitivity under a self-controlled surface.

22

1893 Birth of Dorothy Parker, American writer and wit

1940 Birth of Valerie Harper, American actress

23

1912 Birth of Gene Kelly, American dancer and entertainer

Salad-days
Make an eye-catching salad of marigolds, nasturtiums, borage flowers and mixed salad leaves as part of a birthday lunch or dinner.

24

1899 Birth of Jorge Luis Borges, Argentinian writer

If the twenty-fourth of August be fair and
*   clear,*
Then hope for a prosperous Autumn that
*   year.*
                                    JOHN RAY

25

1930 Birth of Sean Connery, Scottish actor

26

27

28

1828 Birth of Count Leo Tolstoy, Russian author of *War and Peace*

1929 Birth of Jackie Onassis, American editor and widow of President Kennedy

August

Polarity: Virgo is a negative or feminine sign. These signs have a self-repressive and passive tendency.

29

1915 Birth of Ingrid Bergman, Swedish-born American actress

1923 Birth of Sir Richard Attenborough, English film actor, director and producer

1958 Birth of Michael Jackson, American singer

30

1943 Birth of Jean-Claude Killey, French ski champion

31

1928 Birth of James Coburn, American film actor

1949 Birth of Richard Gere, American film actor

Colorful cubes
To add that special touch to a celebratory summer beverage, encapsulate edible flowers such as borage in ice cubes. To ensure that the flowers do not float to the top of the cubes, half fill the ice cube moulds, add the flowers and a little more water. Freeze, then top up with water.

Pimm's cocktail
Stir 1 part *Pimm's No 1 Cup* * with 2 or 3 parts ginger ale or lemonade. Add plenty of ice, a slice of lemon, a slice of orange and borage flowers and leaves, which have a faint cucumber flavor.

* or lemon-lime vodka

September

Birthstone: sapphire

A maiden born when Autumn leaves
Are rustling in September's breeze,
A sapphire on her brow should bind,
'Twill cure diseases of the mind.

ANON

September

1

2

1913 Birth of Alan Ladd, US film actor

3

4

1905 Birth of Mary Renault, English author whose novels were set in ancient Greece

5

1847 Birth of Jesse James, American outlaw

1940 Birth of Raquel Welch, American actress

6

Warm September brings the fruit,
Sportsmen then begin to shoot.
SARA COLERIDGE

7

1533 Birth of Queen Elizabeth I

September

8

1841 Birth of Antonin Dvorak, Czech composer of *The New World Symphony*

1925 Birth of Peter Sellers, British comedian and film actor

9

1935 Birth of Topol, Israeli actor and star of *Fiddler on the Roof*

1941 Birth of Otis Redding, US songwriter and singer

Season of mists and mellow fruitfulness, Close bosom-friend of the maturing sun,
JOHN KEATS

10

Indian summer tomato soup
Add the following to canned tomato juice to taste: finely diced celery, green pepper, cucumber, onion, parsley, basil and seasoning. Chill and serve with a swirl of yogurt or cream if desired.

11

1885 Birth of D H Lawrence, British poet and novelist

12

1888 Birth of Maurice Chevalier, French actor

1913 Birth of Jesse Owens, US track and field athlete

1953 J F Kennedy married Jacqueline Lee Bouvier

13

14

September

15

1890 Birth of Agatha Christie, British novelist and playwright

1945 Birth of Jessye Norman, US concert and opera singer

16

1924 Birth of Lauren Bacall, American actress

1927 Birth of Peter Falk, American actor

17

18

19

1911 Birth of Sir William Golding, English author of *Lord of the Flies*

1933 Birth of David McCallum, Scottish-born actor and star of *The Man from UNCLE*

1948 Birth of Jeremy Irons, British actor

20

1934 Birth of Sophia Loren, Italian film actress

21

1866 Birth of H G Wells, British author

1931 Birth of Larry Hagman, American actor

September

LIBRA
24 September - 23 October
Librans are seekers after perfection and harmony, passionately believing in fairness and equality. Their chief skill lies in the field of diplomacy. Librans are full of charm and style.

22

1902 Birth of John Houseman, writer and actor

23

1930 Birth of Ray Charles, American musician

1949 Birth of Bruce Springsteen, American singer and songwriter

24

1896 Birth of F Scott Fitzgerald, American novelist

Autumn is marching on: even the scarecrows are wearing dead leaves.
OTSUYU NAKAGAWA

25

1931 Birth of Barbara Walters, US television journalist

1944 Birth of Michael Douglas, American actor

1952 Birth of Christopher Reeve, American film actor

26

1898 Birth of George Gershwin, American composer

1948 Birth of Olivia Newton-John, British-born singer and actress

27

28

September

Polarity: Libra is a positive or masculine sign. These signs have a self-expressive and spontaneous tendency.

29

1758 Birth of Horatio Nelson, British admiral

1935 Birth of Jerry Lee Lewis, American pianist-singer

1943 Birth of Lech Walesa, Polish politician

30

1924 Birth of Truman Capote, US author of novels and short stories

Cabbage centerpiece
This is a short-lived but unusual and decorative idea for a table setting. Take a colorful, ornamental cabbage and scatter small flowerheads amongst the leaves, such as brodeia, pelargoniums and pink chrysanthemums.

Red cabbage with apples
1 red cabbage
2oz (¼ cup or 50g) margarine
2 dessert apples, peeled and chopped
1 small onion, peeled and chopped
Seasoning
12 tbsp (1 cup or 170mL) red wine
Grated nutmeg

Finely shred cabbage. Melt margarine in a large pan, add cabbage, apples, onion and seasoning. Cook gently for 5 minutes, turning occasionally. Add wine and nutmeg, cover pan with a tightly-fitting lid and cook until liquid has just evaporated. Serve with pork or goose.

October

Birthstone: opal or pink tourmaline

October's child is born for woe,
And life's vicissitudes must know;
But lay an opal on her breast,
And hope will lull those woes to rest.

ANON

October

1

1928 Birth of Mickey Mouse

1933 Birth of Richard Harris, Irish actor

1935 Birth of Julie Andrews, British actress and singer

2

1895 Birth of Groucho Marx, American comedian and film actor

1904 Birth of Graham Greene, British novelist

1951 Birth of Sting, singer-songwriter and actor

3

1916 Birth of James Herriot, British vet and writer

1925 Birth of Gore Vidal, US author and critic

1941 Birth of Chubby Checker, US singer who introduced the Twist

4

1895 Birth of Buster Keaton, American film actor and director

1924 Birth of Charlton Heston, American film actor

5

1936 Birth of Vaclav Havel, Czechoslovak playwright and President

6

1905 Birth of Helen Wills-Moody, US tennis champion

7

1931 Birth of Desmond Tutu, South African Archbishop and Nobel Peace Prize winner

1955 Birth of Yo Yo Ma, Chinese cellist

1957 Birth of Jayne Torvill, three-times world ice-dance champion with Christopher Dean

October

8

9

1890 Birth of Aimee Semple McPherson, US radio evangelist

1900 Birth of Alaistair Sim, Scottish actor

1940 Birth of John Lennon, British singer-songwriter, member of *The Beatles*

10

1924 Birth of John Clavell, English-born novelist and screenwriter

1930 Birth of Harold Pinter, British playwright

1946 Birth of Ben Vereen, US dancer and actor

11

1884 Birth of Eleanor Roosevelt, wife of 32nd President and writer, civil rights campaigner

12

1492 Columbus discovered the New World

1935 Birth of Luciano Pavarotti, Italian opera singer

13

1925 Birth of Margaret Thatcher, British Prime Minister

1941 Birth of Paul Simon, US singer, songwriter and musician

14

1927 Birth of Roger Moore, British actor

1964 Martin Luther King was awarded the Nobel Peace Prize

October

15

1908 Birth of John Kenneth Galbraith, Canadian economist

1920 Birth of Mario Puzo, US author of *The Godfather*

16

1854 Birth of Oscar Wilde, British writer and wit

1888 Birth of Eugene O'Neil, US playwright

1925 Birth of Angela Lansbury, British-born American actress

17

1918 Birth of Rita Hayworth, American film actress

I saw old Autumn in the misty morn
Stand shadowless like silence.
THOMAS HOOD

18

1926 Birth of Chuck Berry, American singer and composer

1956 Birth of Martina Navratilova, Czech-born American tennis player

19

1931 Birth of John le Carré, British novelist

1987 "Black Monday" on Wall Street wiped out millions on stock markets

20

1884 Birth of Bela Lugosi, Hungarian actor who played *Dracula*

21

October

SCORPIO
24 October - 22 November
Scorpios are highly sensitive and compassionate with a fierce pride and determination. Capable of great patience, they possess a profound insight, but can be deeply cynical.

22

1844 Birth of Sarah Bernhardt, French actress

1943 Birth of Catherine Deneuve, French actress

23

1925 Birth of Johnny Carson, US entertainer and talk show host

1940 Birth of Pelé, Brazilian soccer player

24

1945 The United Nations Charter came into force

United Nation's Day

25

1881 Birth of Pablo Picasso, Spanish artist

26

1942 Birth of Bob Hoskins, British film actor

27

1914 Birth of Dylan Thomas, Welsh writer

1932 Birth of Sylvia Plath, US poet and author of *The Bell Jar*

1939 Birth of John Cleese, British film and television writer, actor and director

28

1914 Birth of Jonas Salk, US developer of polio vaccine

1927 Birth of Cleo Laine, British singer

October

29

1948 Birth of Richard Dreyfuss, US actor

30

1885 Birth of Ezra Pound, US poet

1932 Birth of Louis Malle, French film director

31

1795 Birth of John Keats, English poet

1920 Birth of Dick Francis, British novelist

Bewitching black velvet
Pour equal quantities of chilled champagne and chilled stout simultaneously and slowly into a champagne flute and serve.

Pumpkin scones
10oz (2½ cups or 300g) well-drained
   cooked pumpkin
1oz (2 tbsp or 25g) softened butter
1 tbsp sugar
1 tbsp honey
1 egg
9oz (2¼ cups or 250g) self-raising
   flour
Pinch of salt
1 tsp ground cinnamon
¼ tsp grated nutmeg
2 fl oz (50ml or ¼ cup) milk

Heat oven to 450° F (230°C).
Mash pumpkin. Mix the butter with the sugar and honey. Beat the egg and mix with pumpkin. Add to butter and sugar. Sift flour, salt and spices into a bowl, then fold into pumpkin mixture alternately with the milk. Add more milk, if necessary, to form a soft dough. Knead the dough lightly and pat out to ¾in (2cm) thick. Cut into rounds with a 2in (5cm) cutter. Place on a greased baking sheet and bake for 12-15 minutes.

November

Birthstone: topaz or citrine

Who first comes to this world below
With drear November's fog and snow
Should prize the topaz's amber hue –
Emblem of friends and lovers true.

ANON

November

Element: Scorpio is a water sign. These signs are artistic, emotional and perceptive.

1

1871 Birth of Stephen Crane, US author of *The Red Badge of Courage*

1924 Birth of Jimmy Carter, 39th president of the USA

2

1755 Birth of Marie Antoinette, Queen of France

1913 Birth of Burt Lancaster, American film actor

3

1801 Birth of Vincenzo Bellini, Italian opera composer

1922 Birth of Charles Bronson, American film actor

1957 Laika the dog became the first living creature in space

4

1875 Birth of Will Rogers, US humorist and actor

1916 Birth of Walter Cronkite, US journalist and television anchorman

1937 Birth of Loretta Swit, US actress

5

1913 Birth of Vivien Leigh, British actress

1941 Birth of Elke Sommer, German actress

6

7

1867 Birth of Marie Curie, Polish-French scientist and double Nobel Prize winner

November

8

1900 Birth of Margaret Mitchell, American novelist, author of *Gone with the Wind*

9

1909 Birth of Katharine Hepburn, American actress

10

1925 Birth of Richard Burton, British actor

11

Veterans' Day

12

1929 Birth of Princess Grace of Monaco, former American film actress

13

1850 Birth of Robert Louis Stevenson, Scottish author

14

1840 Birth of Claude Monet, French painter

1948 Birth of Charles, the Prince of Wales

November

22

1958 Birth of Jamie Lee Curtis, American film actress

1967 Birth of Boris Becker, German tennis player

23

1887 Birth of Boris Karloff, English-American film actor

24

1864 Birth of Henri de Toulouse-Lautrec, French artist

1868 Birth of Scott Joplin, US ragtime pianist and composer

25

1844 Birth of Karl Benz, German inventor of the motor car

1914 Birth of Joe DiMaggio, American baseball great

26

1922 Birth of Charles Schulz, US cartoonist who created *Peanuts*

27

1942 Birth of Jimi Hendrix, US guitarist and singer

28

1820 Birth of Friedrich Engels, German socialist and associate of Karl Marx

November

Polarity: Sagittarius is a positive or masculine sign. These signs have a self-expressive and spontaneous tendency.

29

1832 Birth of Louisa May Alcott, American novelist, author of *Little Women*

30

1835 Birth of Mark Twain, US humorist and novelist

1874 Birth of Winston Churchill, British statesman and writer

Mixed spice pot pourri
Mix together the following ingredients in a large bowl: 2 cups dried lavender flowers, 2 cups dried rose petals, 1 cup lemon verbena leaves, 1 cup cornflower petals, $\frac{1}{2}$ cup powdered orris root, 1 tbsp ground allspice, 1 tbsp ground cinnamon, 1 tbsp ground cloves. Add a few drops of essential oil. Place in paper bag, seal and shake. Store for 6 weeks.

Orange and clove pomander
Make a natural, aromatic pomander by scoring the rind of an orange into equal segments. Stick the orange with whole cloves to make a pleasing design, then hang by a length of decorative ribbon. This kind of pomander is a traditional Christmas decoration in Scandinavia.

December

Birthstone: turquoise or zircon

If cold December gave you birth,
The month of snow and ice and mirth,
Place on your hand a turquoise blue,
Success will bless whate'er you do.

ANON

December

1

1935 Birth of Woody Allen, American actor, writer, producer and director

2

Christmas is coming, the geese are getting fat,
Please to put a penny in the old man's hat;
If you haven't got a penny, a ha'penny will do,
If you haven't got a ha'penny, God bless you.
                                    OLD ENGLISH CAROL

3

1857 Birth of Joseph Conrad, Polish-born author of *Heart of Darkness*

1967 First successful heart transplant operation performed

4

5

1901 Birth of Walt Disney, American film maker

6

Winter warmer
Stick 3 cloves into an orange slice. Stir 3 tbsp rum and 1 tsp brown sugar together in the bottom of a handled mug. Add a lemon slice and very hot water to fill the mug. Stir with a cinnamon stick.

7

We shall hear
The rain and wind beat dark December
                                    SHAKESPEARE

December

8

1865 Birth of Jean Sibelius, Finnish composer

1894 Birth of James Thurber, US humorist, cartoonist and writer

1953 Birth of Kim Basinger, American actress

9

1916 Birth of Kirk Douglas, American film actor

1929 Birth of John Cassavetes, US actor and director

1952 Birth of Joan Armatrading, English singer and songwriter

10

1830 Birth of Emily Dickinson, US poet

The sun, that brief December day,
Rose cheerless over hills of gray,
And, darkly circled, gave at noon
A sadder light than waning moon.
J G WHITTIER

11

1918 Birth of Aleksandr Solzhenitsyn, Soviet writer

12

1915 Birth of Frank Sinatra, American singer, actor and composer

1941 Birth of Dionne Warwick, American singer

13

14

1911 Norwegian Roald Amundsen became the first explorer to reach the South Pole

1935 Birth of Lee Remick, American actress

December

15

1892 Birth of John Paul Getty, American billionaire

16

1775 Birth of Jane Austen, English novelist

1899 Birth of Noel Coward, British playwright, actor and composer

1901 Birth of Margaret Mead, American anthropologist

17

1903 Wright Brothers made the first heavier than air flight

18

1916 Birth of Betty Grable, American film actress

1947 Birth of Steven Spielberg, US film director

Green Christmas, white Easter.
GERMAN PROVERB

19

1902 Birth of Sir Ralph Richardson, British actor

1915 Birth of Edith Piaf, French singer and actress

20

21

December

CAPRICORN
22 December - 20 January
Capricorns may experience hardship in
early life but their resourcefulness
makes them self-sufficient survivors.
Often difficult to get to know, they are
down-to-earth and highly responsible.

22

1907 Birth of Dame Peggy Ashcroft,
British actress

23

Rum truffles
Melt 3oz (⅓ cup or 85g) plain (dark)
chocolate over a pan of hot water. Add
an egg yolk, 1 tbsp rum and 1 tsp cream.
Beat until thick. Leave to cool, then form
into balls and roll in chocolate
vermicelli. Chill.

24

Christmas Eve

'Twas the night before Christmas, when
all through the house
Not a creature was stirring, not even a
mouse.

C C MOORE

25

Christmas Day

26

Boxing Day

27

1901 Birth of Marlene Dietrich,
German-born American film actress

1948 Birth of Gérard Depardieu,
French actor

28

1905 Birth of Earl 'Fatha' Hines, US
jazz pianist

1934 Birth of Maggie Smith, British
actress

December

29

1936 Birth of Mary Tyler Moore, US actress

30

1865 Birth of Rudyard Kipling, British writer

31

New Year's Eve

1937 Birth of Anthony Hopkins, British actor

1943 Birth of Ben Kingsley, British actor

1943 Birth of John Denver, American singer-songwriter

Highland fling
5 tbsp (⅓ cup or 70ml) Scotch whisky
1 tsp honey
2 tsp lime juice
2 tbsp (30ml) Drambuie

Stir the Scotch, honey and lime juice in a mug. Warm the Drambuie in a ladle and ignite it. Pour the burning liquid into the mug. Stir and drink immediately.

Hangover cocktail
Shake together 4 parts milk, 1 part brandy, 1 tsp sugar and a dash of Angostura bitters in a cocktail shaker. Pour into a chilled tumbler and top up with soda water.

Chinese Astrology

RAT

31 January 1900 – 18 February 1901
18 February 1912 – 5 February 1913
 5 February 1924 – 24 January 1925
24 January 1936 – 10 February 1937
10 February 1948 – 28 January 1949
28 January 1960 – 14 February 1961
16 January 1972 – 2 February 1973
 2 February 1984 – 19 February 1985
19 February 1996 – 6 February 1997

Rats are charming creatures, contrary to their reputation in the animal kingdom. Amusing and intelligent, they love socializing and attract a wide circle of friends. However, these relationships can be short-lived, since Rats adore gossip.

Although they can be quick to anger, Rat people are able to conceal their negative feelings beneath a calm, cool exterior.

Rats are acquisitive, salting away their money in an effort to feel secure. They are ambitious and persistent, often being successful in business enterprises. However, in this context as in their personal lives, Rats need constant communication and support. They thrive on a frenzy of activity in a variety of fields, in both work and recreational spheres.

OX

19 February 1901 – 7 February 1902
 6 February 1913 – 25 January 1914
25 January 1925 – 12 February 1926
11 February 1937 – 30 January 1938
29 January 1949 – 16 February 1950
15 February 1961 – 4 February 1962
 3 February 1973 – 22 January 1974
20 February 1985 – 8 February 1986
 7 February 1997 – 27 January 1998

Ox people are placid and stable, utterly reliable and tenacious. They are true survivors, doggedly plodding on through life's obstacles and pitfalls to achieve their chosen aims.

Ox people are careful about who they take into their confidence, but once you have earned their trust, you will enjoy their sympathy, sound advice and willingness to give constructive help when the situation arises. Although tolerant and easy-going, it is dangerous to push the Ox too far; he or she makes a formidable and long-lived enemy.

No strangers to domesticity, Ox people make excellent parents and caring, loyal partners. You may find them looking after the elderly, large numbers of children or the sick.

TIGER

 8 February 1902 – 28 January   1903
26 January 1914 – 13 February 1915
13 February 1926 – 1 February 1927
31 January 1938 – 18 February 1939
17 February 1950 – 5 February 1951
 5 February 1962 – 24 January   1963
23 January 1974 – 10 February 1975
 9 February 1986 – 28 January   1987
28 January 1998 – 15 February 1999

Tiger people are powerful and courageous in line with their animal counterparts. Together with their capacity for original, creative thought, Tigers are natural leaders. However, while occupying their elevated positions in society, Tiger people can be selfish and stubborn, exercising an unwillingness to take heed of or trust others beneath them. They have a rebellious streak and tend to resent their elders or anyone in a position of authority above them.

Tigers can be wild creatures, lacking in stability and prone to restlessness. Quick to become bored, they thrive on variety and constant challenge. Tigers are not easily tamed; they value their freedom and independence too much.

Chinese Astrology

HARE

29 January 1903 – 15 February 1904
14 February 1915 – 2 February 1916
 2 February 1927 – 22 January 1928
19 January 1939 – 7 February 1940
 6 February 1951 – 26 January 1952
25 January 1963 – 12 February 1964
11 February 1975 – 30 January 1976
29 January 1987 – 16 February 1988
16 February 1999 – 4 February 2000

Hares are sensitive and intuitive creatures that love the company of others, seeking the warmth and security of a one-to-one relationship. They make responsive companions, tactful, respectful and sympathetic. Hares will do anything to keep the peace; they will back off at the first sign of trouble.

Naturally reserved, Hares may withdraw into the safety of their own private, untouchable world. They are highly cautious and seek the tranquility and security of a real home above all things. Often lucky financially, Hares have an uncanny sense for picking a winner and make good gamblers, disciplined as they are by their innate caution.

DRAGON

16 February 1904 – 3 February 1905
 3 February 1916 – 22 January 1917
23 January 1928 – 9 February 1929
 8 February 1940 – 26 January 1941
27 January 1952 – 13 February 1953
13 February 1964 – 1 February 1965
31 January 1976 – 17 February 1977
17 February 1988 – 5 February 1989

Dragons are larger than life, befitting their mythological status in Chinese astrology. They will attract attention in any situation, even though it may not always be of a positive nature! Flamboyant, glamorous and strong-willed, the Dragon draws people to him or her like a magnet.

Full of energy, drive and ambition, Dragons are highly visible in society as politicians, film stars, pop stars and entrepreneurs – always in the forefront of their chosen fields. However, prepare yourself for the Dragon's lack of consideration for others. He or she can be unfaithful or unreliable but you will doubtless be persuaded to give them a second or more chance, such is their attraction.

SNAKE

 4 February 1905 – 24 January 1906
23 January 1917 – 10 February 1918
10 February 1929 – 29 January 1930
27 January 1941 – 14 February 1942
14 February 1953 – 2 February 1954
22 February 1965 – 20 January 1966
18 February 1977 – 6 February 1978
 6 February 1989 – 26 January 1990

Snakes are often physically attractive but in addition they have a flair for creating just the right look for any occasion by judiciously applying a few individual and creative touches. They have a special gift for recognizing potential where few other people would, and helping to fulfil it to great effect. This trait helps Snakes to succeed in business.

Snakes have a subtle way of leading people into thinking that they are supremely knowledgeable in whatever field suits their purpose at the time. However, they would not stoop to telling downright lies.

Often romantic, snakes are attentive to the changing moods and appearance of their nearest and dearest, although they will quickly become morose if this attention is not reciprocated.

Chinese Astrology

HORSE

25 January 1906 – 12 February 1907
11 February 1918 – 31 January 1919
30 January 1930 – 16 February 1931
15 February 1942 – 4 February 1943
 3 February 1954 – 23 January 1955
21 January 1966 – 8 February 1967
 7 February 1978 – 27 January 1979
27 January 1990 – 14 February 1991

Horses are popular, friendly creatures but can have a fiery, rebellious latent tendency. They are physically energetic, strong and enduring, and will invariably work hard at any job. However, they may be over-enthusiastic and single-minded about a pet project and behave somewhat impetuously and pig-headedly.

Horses are gregarious people and enjoy entertainment on a large scale. They enjoy spending money, for instance on expensive clothes, but they do not squander their financial resources. Many of them put their boundless energy into travel. Horse people are prone to falling hopelessly in love and become blind to the world outside.

SHEEP

13 February 1907 – 1 February 1908
 1 February 1919 – 19 February 1920
17 February 1931 – 5 February 1932
 5 February 1943 – 24 January 1944
24 January 1955 – 11 February 1956
 9 February 1967 – 29 January 1968
28 January 1979 – 15 February 1980
15 February 1991 – 3 February 1992

Sheep are gentle, selfless creatures – you will find many of them in the caring professions. They are often artistic but tend to follow an established tradition rather than create an original style. Consequently, they make skilled craftspeople. In fact, in all spheres of life Sheep people, like the animals they are named after, are followers rather than leaders. They often lack a sense of direction and therefore can become lost and confused in life if they do not receive strong but kindly guidance. Left to their own devices, Sheep can be irresponsible and impractical.

Sheep people can be great peacemakers, able to defuse an explosive situation with their considerable tact and diplomacy. They value security above all else.

MONKEY

 2 February 1908 – 21 January 1909
20 February 1920 – 7 February 1921
 6 February 1932 – 25 January 1933
25 January 1944 – 12 February 1945
12 February 1956 – 30 January 1957
30 January 1968 – 16 February 1969
16 February 1980 – 4 February 1981
 4 February 1992 – 22 January 1993

Monkeys are multi-talented people, being quick of wit and highly adaptable. However, in view of their light-hearted natures and great sense of humour, their worth can be underestimated by other people who refuse to take them seriously. If valued and encouraged, Monkeys can be extremely successful in business with their adeptness at making deals.

Although delightful company, Monkeys can be unreliable and less than honest, even double-dealing in personal relationships. Therefore, the Monkey may find his or her associations short-lived and unfulfilled. In fact, Monkeys tend to have many different relationships in their lives before establishing a deep and lasting liaison.

Monkeys are often gifted story-tellers, being drawn to the world of fantasy.

Chinese Astrology

ROOSTER

22 January 1909 – 9 February 1910
8 February 1921 – 27 January 1922
26 January 1933 – 13 February 1934
13 February 1945 – 1 February 1946
31 January 1957 – 17 February 1958
17 February 1969 – 5 February 1970
5 February 1981 – 24 January 1982
23 January 1993 – 9 February 1994

Roosters are dilligent, efficient and deeply committed, often working long and hard to achieve their chosen goals. However, they are prone to taking on more work than they can cope with and experiencing bitter disappointment when they fail. Roosters like to work on their own in their own way and strongly react against any outside interference. They can be overbearing and bossy in their frustration with less-capable colleagues or partners.

Roosters have a reputation for being forthright, but their honesty to the point of bluntness can cause them to lose friends.

Inclined to the eccentric, Roosters adore adventure and make intrepid explorers of the world at large.

DOG

10 February 1910 – 29 January 1911
28 January 1922 – 15 February 1923
14 February 1934 – 3 February 1935
2 February 1946 – 21 January 1947
18 February 1958 – 7 February 1959
6 February 1970 – 26 January 1971
25 January 1982 – 12 February 1983
10 February 1994 – 30 January 1995

Dogs are blessed with many of the finer traits of human nature. They are faithful and reliable, just like their animal counterparts, hard-working and dutiful. They are always anxious to give of their best. However, Dogs can be rather conservative, reluctant to embrace new ideas and to develop. They can also be slow to learn, thus trying the patience of other signs.

Dogs need close contact with other people. They are sympathetic, supportive, forgiving and discreet in human relationships. However, if a Dog takes a dislike to you, he or she can be highly critical and sarcastic. Dogs are not known for their romantic natures.

Dogs need a good deal of encouragement to fulfil their potential. Unfortunately, some suffer from a lack of belief in themselves.

PIG

30 January 1911 – 17 February 1912
16 February 1923 – 4 February 1924
4 February 1935 – 23 January 1936
22 January 1947 – 9 February 1948
8 February 1959 – 27 January 1960
27 January 1971 – 15 January 1972
13 February 1983 – 1 February 1984
31 January 1995 – 18 February 1996

Pig people set a worthy example to the other signs. They are caring of others, particularly their families which are of paramount importance in their lives. They have an unshakeable faith in human nature and are staggeringly tolerant of the weaknesses of others.

Pigs are highly industrious, taking great pains to carry out any task thoroughly and properly. They take great pride in their endeavours. Almost fanatically efficient and tidy, Pig people want to succeed only on the basis of their own merits and hard labour.

The Pig may have few friends but they will be of the lifelong variety.

Anniversaries

1st	Paper or cotton
2nd	Cotton or paper
3rd	Leather
4th	Silk or flowers
5th	Wood
6th	Iron or candy
7th	Copper or wool
8th	Bronze or rubber
9th	Pottery
10th	Tin
11th	Steel
12th	Linen
13th	Lace
14th	Ivory
15th	Crystal
20th	China
25th	Silver
30th	Pearl
35th	Coral
40th	Ruby
45th	Sapphire
50th	Gold
55th	Emerald
60th	Diamond
75th	Diamond

Symbolism of Gemstones

Amethyst: humility, sincerity and prevention of drunkenness

Aquamarine: courage and energy

Bloodstone: courage and wisdom

Carbuncle: lucky in love

Crystal: purity and simplicity

Diamond: innocence, success, conjugal affection, unshakeable faith.

Emerald: safety in child-bearing, lucky in love, tranquility

Garnet: constancy and truth

Moonstone: drives away nightmares

Onyx: sincerity

Opal: unlucky unless it is the fiancée's birthstone, reflects every mood

Pearl: beautiful bride, but signifies tears

Peridot: kind to husband

Ruby: freedom from care, chastity, glory

Sapphire: chastity and hope

Sardonyx: secures marital happiness

Topaz: cure for sleeplessness, fidelity

Turquoise: prevents arguments in matrimony, love and riches

Say it with Flowers

FLOWERS – both cultivated and those with a native nature – have become associated with sentiments, often with the purpose of conveying amorous thoughts. In the 1600s in Constantinople (what became Istanbul), flowers gained meanings which enabled lovers to convey messages to each other without having to write or talk.

This language of flowers was introduced to Europe by Lady Mary Wortley Montagu, a celebrated letter-writer and society poet who, in 1716, accompanied her husband to the Turkish Court in Istanbul. During her stay, she sent a Turkish love letter to England which interpreted the meanings of some plants, flowers and spices. The wonder of flowers, she proposed, was that words and messages of love – even altercations – could be passed in a refined and subtle manner without *'inking the fingers'*. She returned to England in 1718, bringing with her additional information about the language of flowers.

The passing of messages via the floral code was then taken up by the French, only to return later to England during the reign of Queen Victoria through Madame de la Tour's book *Le Langage des Fleurs*. However, many of the phrases contained in this book were risqué and too lusty for gentile Victorian society. The language was therefore toned down in English books on the subject published at that time. To this day, for many people saying it with flowers continues to signify romance, enchantment and a special consideration.

More than 800 flowers have special meanings associated with them. Indeed, there are over 30 for roses alone. Messages can become quite complex when several flowers are presented in a bouquet. For example, one formed of the oak-leaved geranium, gillyflower and heliotrope, with a leaf of the virginia creeper would mean: *I offer true friendship, affection and devotion*, while another of monkshood, mountain ash and blue violet conveys: *Danger is near; be prudent and faithful*. Other bouquets, perhaps of red poppy, clematis, harebell and bound with virginia creeper, would suggest: *I offer consolation. You have mental beauty. I submit to you*. A combination of mistletoe, hawthorn and heliotrope turned to the right means: *I surmount difficulties. I hope. I turn to thee*.

The way in which flowers were worn and presented had a meaning in addition to the sentiments attached to individual flowers. A flower bent towards the right would signify *I*, while one extending to the left would mean *you*. Therefore, a red rosebud leaning to the left would say: *You are pure and lovely*. Foliage had an additional significance, leaves meaning hope, thorns danger. Therefore, a rose with the thorns plucked off but the leaves left intact would convey *hopeful love and confidence*.

The language is further enriched by the hand – left or right – that proffers the flowers, as well the one that receives it. An affirmative is suggested by the right hand, while the left one indicates a negative. Thus a provence rose offered by the right hand underlines the sentiment *My heart is in flames* and, if received by a right hand, would give satisfaction to the giver.

If flowers could not be presented personally, they were sent in boxes tied with ribbons, and these too held a message, depending on where the knot was tied.

David Squire

A

A beauty
Orchis

A belle
Orchis

A heart ignorant of love
White rosebud

A smile
Sweet william

A token
Ox-eye daisy, laurestina

Absence
Wormwood

Abuse not
Crocus

Acknowledgment
Canterbury bell

Activity
Thyme

Adversity, energy in
Camomile

Admiration
Amethyst

Adoration
Dwarf sunflower

Adresses rejected
Ice plant

Advice
Rhubarb

Affectation
Morning glory

Affection
Mossy saxifrage, pear, sorrel

Affection, bonds of
Gillyflower

Affection, enduring
Gorse

Afterthought
Michaelmas Daisy

Age
Guelder rose

Agreement
Straw

Alas! for my poor heart
Deep red carnation

Always lovely
Indian double pink

Am I forgotten?
Holly

Ambition
Mountain laurel

Amiability
Jasmine

Anticipation
Gooseberry

Anxiety, tranquilize my
Christmas rose

Anxious and trembling
Red columbine

Appointed meeting
Everlasting pea

Ardent love
Balsam

Ardor
Cuckoo plant, arum lily

Argument
Fig

Artifice
Acanthus

Assiduous to please
Sprig of ivy with tendrils

Assignation
Pimpernel

Attachment
Indian jasmine

Austerity
Common thistle

Avarice
Scarlet auricula

Aversion
Indian single pink

B

Bantering
Southernwood

Bashful shame
Deep red rose

Bashfulness
Peony

Be mine
Four-leaved clover

Beautiful, call me not
Unique rose

Beautiful eyes
Variegated tulip

Beauty
Parti-coloured daisy, full red rose

Beauty, a
Orchis

Beauty always new
China rose

Beauty and prosperity
Red-leaved rose

Beauty, capricious
Lady's slipper, musk rose

Beauty, delicate
Hibiscus

Beauty, divine
American cowslip

Beauty, lasting
Stock

Beauty, mental
Clematis

Beauty, pensive
Laburnum

Beauty, rustic
French honeysuckle

Beauty, unconscious
Burgundy rose

Beauty, unfading
Gillyflower

Belief
Passion-flower

Belle, a
Orchis

Benevolence
Potato

Betrayal
Judas tree

Beware
Oleander

Beware of excess
Saffron

Blackness
Ebony

Bluntness
Borage

Blushes
Marjoram

Boaster, a
Hydrangea

Boldness
Pink

Bonds
Convolvulus

Bonds of affection
Gillyflower

Bravery
Oak leaves

Bulk
Water melon, gourd

Bury me amid Nature's beauties
Persimmon

C

Call me not beautiful
Unique rose

Capricious beauty
Lady's slipper, musk rose

Change
Pimpernel

Changeable disposition
Rye grass

Charity
Turnip

Charming
Cluster of musk roses

Chaste love
Acacia

Cheerfulness in old age
American Starwort

Cheerfulness under adversity
Chrysanthemum

Childishness
Buttercup

Chivalry
Great yellow daffodil

Cleanliness
Hyssop

Coldheartedness
Lettuce

Color of my life
Coral honeysuckle

Come down
Jacob's ladder

Comforting
Scarlet geranium

Compassion
Allspice

Concealed love
Motherwort

Concealed merit
Coriander

Confession of love
Moss rosebud

Confidence
Lilac polyanthus

Conjugal love
Lime

Consolation
Red poppy

Cordiality
Peppermint

Counterfeit
Mock orange

Crime
Tamarisk

Criticism
Cucumber

Cure
Balm of gilead

Cure for heartache
Cranberry, swallow-wort

Curiosity
Sycamore

D

Danger
Rhododendron, monkshood

Dangerous pleasures
Tuberose

Dauntlessness
Sea lavender

Death
Cypress

Deceit
Flytrap, dogsbane

Deceitful charms
Thorn-apple

Deception
White cherry

Declaration of love
Red tulip

Decrease of love
Yellow sweet-brier, yellow rose

Dejection
Lichen

Delay
Eupatorium

Delicacy
Cornflower

Delicate beauty
Hibiscus

Departure
Sweet pea

Despair
Cypress and marigold

Devotion
Heliotrope

Difficulties, I surmount
Mistletoe

Dignity
Cloves, laurel-leaved magnolia

Disappointment
Carolina syringa

Discretion
Lemon blossoms, maidenhair

Disdain
Yellow carnation, rue

Distinction
Cardinal flower

Distrust
Lavender

Divine beauty
American cowslip

Do me justice
Sweet chestnut tree

Do not abuse
Saffron

Domestic industry
Flax

ℰ

Early attachment
Thornless rose

Early friendship
Blue periwinkle

Early youth
Primrose

Education
Cherry tree

Elegance and grace
Yellow jasmine

Elegance, mature
Pomegranate flower

Elevation
Scotch fir

Enchantment
Holly herb

Enduring affection
Gorse

Energy in adversity
Camomile

Envy
Crane's bill, bramble

Esteem
Garden sage

Esteem and love
Strawberry tree

Esteem but not love
Spiderwort

Estranged love
Lotus flower

Evanescent pleasure
Poppy

Excellence, perfect
Strawberry

Excellence, unpretending
Camellia japonica

Excess, beware of
Saffron

Expectation
Anemone

Expected meeting
Nutmeg, geraniums

Extent
Gourd

Extinguished hopes
Major convolvulus

Extravagance, fantastic
Scarlet poppy

Eyes, beautiful
Variegated tulip

ℱ

Faithfulness
Blue violet, heliotrope

Falsehood
Yellow lily

Fame
Tulip

Fantastic extravagance
Scarlet poppy

Farewell
Michaelmas daisy

Fascination
Carnation, honesty

Fashion
Lady's mantle

Fate
Hemp

Feasting
Parsley

Fecundity
Hollyhock

Female ambition
White hollyhock

Female fidelity
Speedwell

Festivity
Parsley

Fickleness
Pink larkspur

Fidelity in love
Lemon blossoms

Filial love
Virgin's bower

Fine arts, the
Acanthus

Finesse
Sweet william

Fire
Fleur-de-luce

First emotions of love
Purple lilac

Fitness
Sweet flag

Flame
Fleur-de-lis, iris

Flee away
Pennyroyal

Folly
Columbine

Foolishness
Pomegranate

Foresight
Holly

Forget me not
Forget-me-not

Forsaken
Garden anemone, laburnum

Forsaken love
Creeping willow

Fraternal love
Woodbine

Freedom
Water willow

Freshness
Damask rose

Friends, thoughts of absent
Zinnia

Friendship
Rose acacia

G

Gaiety
Butterfly orchis, yellow lily

Gain
Cabbage

Gallantry
A nosegay, sweet william

Generosity
Orange tree

Generous and devoted affection
French honeysuckle

Genius
Plane tree

Gentility
Geranium, pompon rose

Girlhood
White rosebud

Gladness
Myrrh

Gladness, youthful
Spring crocus

Glory
Bay tree, laurel

Good wishes
Sweet basil

Goodness
Mercury

Grace
Multiflora rose

Grace and elegance
Yellow jasmine

Gracefulness
Birch tree

Grandeur
Ash tree

Grief
Harebell, marigold

H

Happiness, return of
Lily of the valley

Happy love
Bridal rose

Hatred
Basil

Haughtiness
Purple larkspur, tall sunflower

Health
Iceland moss

Heart's mystery, the
Crimson polyanthus

Heartlessness
Hydrangea

Hidden worth
Coriander

Honesty
Honesty

Hope
Flowering almond, hawthorn, snowdrop

Hope extinguished
Major convolvulus

Hope in adversity
Spruce pine

Hopeless love
Yellow tulip

Hopeless, not heartless
Love-lies-bleeding

Hospitality
Oak tree

Humility
Broom, small bindweed, field lilac

I

I am too happy
Cape jasmine

I am worthy of you
White rose

I am your captive
Peach blossom

I aspire to thy smile
Daily rose

I attach myself to you
Indian jasmine

I change but in death
Bay leaf

I declare against you
Liquorice

I desire a return of affection
Jonquil

I die if neglected
Laurestina

I engage you for the next dance
Ivy geranium

I feel your kindness
Flax

I have a message for you
Iris

I live for thee
Cedar leaf

I love
Red chrysanthemum

I surmount difficulties
Mistletoe

I will not answer hastily
Monthly honeysuckle

I will not survive you
Black mulberry

Imagination
Lupin

Immortality
Amaranth

Impatience
Yellow balsam

Impatient resolves
Red balsam

Inconstancy
Evening primrose

Inconstancy in love
Wild honeysuckle

Incorruptible
Cedar of lebanon

Independence
Wild plum tree, white oak

Indifference
Candytuft, mustard seed

Indiscretion
Almond tree

Ingenuity
Pencil-leaved geranium

Ingratitude
Buttercup, wild ranunculus

Injustice
Hop

Innocence
White daisy, white violet

Innocence, youthful
White lilac

Insincerity
Foxglove

Insinuation
Great bindweed

Inspiration
Angelica

Instability
Dahlia

Ireland
Shamrock

J

Jealousy
French marigold, yellow rose

Jest
Southernwood

Joy
Wood sorrel

Joys to come
Celandine

Justice, do me
Sweet chestnut tree

Justice shall be done to you
Coltsfoot

K

Keep your promises
Plum tree

Knowledge, useful
Parsley

L

Lamentation
Aspen tree

Lasting beauty
Stock

Lasting pleasure
Everlasting pea

Levity
Larkspur

Life
Lucerne

Lightheartedness
Shamrock

Lightness
Larkspur

Longevity
Fig

Love
Blue violet, myrtle, rose

Love in idleness
Wild violet

Love is dangerous
Carolina rose

Love of nature
Magnolia

Love returned
Ambrosia

Love's oracle
Dandelion

Love, a heart ignorant of
White rosebud

Love, ambassador of
Cabbage rose

Love, ardent
Balsam

Love, chaste
Acacia

Love, confession of
Moss rosebud

Love, declaration of
Red tulip

Love, estranged
Lotus flower

Love, forsaken
Creeping willow

Love, only deserve my
Campion rose

Love, platonic
Rose acacia

Love, pure and ardent
Double red pink

Love, secret
Toothwort, yellow acacia

Love, slighted
Yellow chrysanthemum

Love, sweet and secret
Honey flower

Love, the first emotions of
Purple lilac

Lovely, thou art all that is
Austrian rose

Love, true
Forget-me-not

Lowliness
Bramble

Majesty
Crown imperial, imperial lily

Malevolence
Lobelia

Marriage
Ivy

Maternal affection
Cinquefoil

Maternal love
Moss

Maternal tenderness
Wood sorrel

Mature elegance
Pomegranate flower

Meekness
Birch

Meeting, an appointed
Everlasting pea

Meeting, an expected
Nutmeg, geranium

Melancholy
Dark geranium, cypress and marigold

Memory, pleasures of
White periwinkle

Mental beauty
Clematis

Merit, concealed
Coriander

Merit, reward of
Bay wreath

Message
Iris

Modesty
White violet, white lilac

Modesty and purity
White lily

Mourning
Weeping willow, cypress

Music
Oats, reeds

My best days are past
Meadow saffron

My compliments
Iris

My heart is in flames
Provence rose

Nature, love of
Magnolia

Neatness
Broom

Night
Minor convolvulus

Old age
Tree of life

Only deserve my love
Campion rose

Ornament
Hornbeam tree

Painting
Auricula

Parental affection
Sorrel

Passion
White dittany, yellow iris

Patience
Dock, ox eye

Patriotism
Nasturtium

Peace
Olive branch

Pensive beauty
Laburnum

Pensiveness
Cowslip

Perfected loveliness
White camellia japonica

Perform your promise
Plum tree

Perplexity
Love-in-a-mist

Perseverance
Canary grass, swamp magnolia

Piety, steadfast
Wild geranium

Pity
Pine

Platonic love
Rose acacia

Play
Hyacinth

Pleasant recollections
White periwinkle

Pleasure and pain
Dog rose

Pleasure, evanescent
Poppy

Pleasure, lasting
Everlasting pea

Pleasures of memory
White periwinkle

Poetry
Eglantine

Poverty
Evergreen clematis

Power
Cress

Precaution
Golden rod

Precocity
May rose

Prediction
Prophetic marigold

Presumption
Snapdragon

Pretension
Spiked willow herb

Prettiness
Pompon rose

Pride
Amaryllis

Promptness
Ten-week stock

Prosperity
Beech tree, wheat

Prudence
Mountain ash

Pure and ardent love
Double red pink

Pure and lovely
Red rosebud

Pure love
Single red pink

Purity
White lilac

Purity and sweetness
White lily

R

Recall
Silver-leaved geranium

Reconciliation
Filbert, hazel

Refusal
Striped carnation, variegated pink

Regard
Daffodil

Relieve my anxiety
Christmas rose

Religious superstition
Aloe, passion-flower

Remembrance
Rosemary, forget-me-not

Remorse
Bramble, raspberry

Rendezvous
Chickweed

Reserve
Maple

Resolution
Purple columbine

Restoration
Persicaria

Retaliation
Scotch thistle

Return of happiness
Lily of the valley

Revenge
Birdsfoot trefoil

Reverie
Flowering fern

Reward of merit
Bay wreath

Reward of virtue
Garland of roses

Riches
Corn

Rivalry
Rocket

Rupture of a contract
Broken straw

Rural happiness
Yellow violet

Rustic beauty
French honeysuckle

Rustic oracle
Dandelion

S

Sadness
Dead leaves, yew

Safety
Traveller's joy

Satire
Prickly pear

Secret love
Toothwort, yellow acacia

Self-esteem
Poet's narcissus

Sensitiveness
Mimosa

Sensuality
Spanish jasmine

Sentiment, warmth of
Spearmint

Separation
Carolina jasmine

Severity
Branch of thorns

Shame
Peony

Sharpness
Barberry

Shyness
Vetch

Sickness
Anemone, zephyr flower

Silence
Belladonna (deadly nightshade)

Silliness
Fool's parsley

Simplicity
American sweet-brier

Sincerity
Fern, honesty

Slander
Stinging nettle

Sleep
White poppy

Slighted love
Yellow chrysanthemum

Splendid beauty
Amarylis

Steadfast piety
Wild geranium

Stoicism
Box tree

Strength
Cedar, fennel

Surprise
Truffle

Susceptibility
Passion-flower

Suspicion
Mushroom

Sweet and secret love
Honey flower

Sympathy
Balm, thrift

T

Talent
White pink

Taste
Scarlet fuchsia

Tears
Helenium

Temperance
Azalea

Temptation
Apple, quince

The color of my fate
Coral honeysuckle

The fine arts
Acanthus

The first emotions of love
Purple lilac

The heart's mystery
Crimson polyanthus

The witching soul of music
Oats

Thoughts
Pansy

Thoughts of absent friends
Zinnia

Thy frown will kill me
Currant

Ties
Tendrils of climbing plants

Time
White poplar

Timidity
Amaryllis

Token, a
Ox-eye daisy, laurestina

Tranquilize my anxiety
Christmas rose

Tranquility
Stonecrop

Transient impressions
Withered white rose

Transport of joy
Cape jasmine

True friendship
Oak-leaved geranium

True love
Forget-me-not

Truth
White chrysanthemum, woody nightshade

U

Unanimity
Phlox

Unbelief
Judas tree

Uncertainty
Convolvulus

Unchangeable
Globe amaranth

Unconscious
Red daisy

Unconscious beauty
Burgundy rose

Unexpected meeting
Lemon geranium

Unfading beauty
Gillyflower

Unfortunate love
Scabious

Unity
White and red rose together

Unpretending excellence
Camellia japonica

Useful knowledge
Parsley

Uselessness
Meadowsweet

V

Variety
Aster, mundi rose

Victory
Palm

Virtue
Mint

Virtue, domestic
Sage

Virtue, reward of
Garland of roses

Voraciousness
Lupin

Vulgar-minded
African marigold

W

War
York rose

Warmth of sentiment
Spearmint

Watchfulness
Dame violet

Widowhood
Sweet scabious

Win me and wear me
Lady's slipper

Winning grace
Cowslip

Winter
Guelder rose

Wisdom
White mulberry

Wish, a
Foxglove

Wit
Ragged robin

Witchcraft
Nightshade

Woman's love
Carnation, carnation pink

Worth beyond beauty
Sweet alyssum

Y

You are perfect
Pine apple

You are radiant with charms
Ranunculus

You are young and beautiful
Red rosebud

You occupy my thoughts
Pansy, purple violet

You please all
Branch of currants

You will be my death
Hemlock

Your looks freeze me
Ice plant

Your presence revives me
Rosemary

Your purity equals your loveliness
Orange blossoms

Your qualities, like your charms, are unequalled
Peach

Youth, early
Primrose

Z

Zealousness
Elder

Zest
Lemon